UPDATED EDITION

Guess What!

Pupil's Book 5
with eBook

British English

Susannah Reed with Kay Bentley
Series Editor: Lesley Koustaff

CAMBRIDGE

Contents

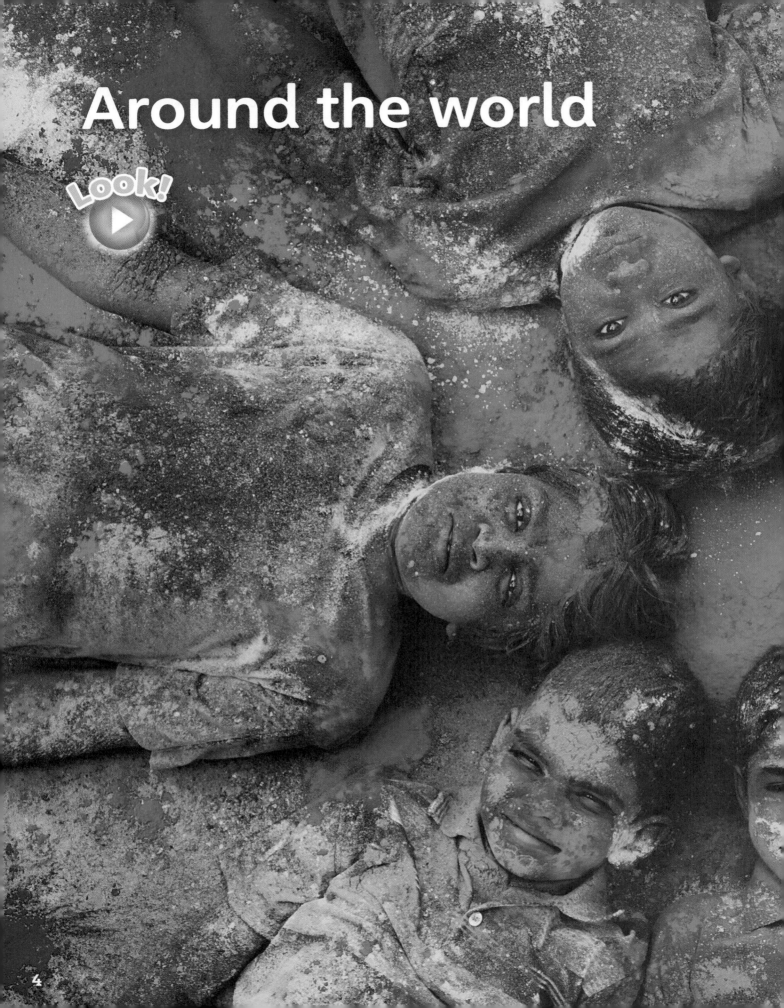

Around the world

Look!

Guess What!

1 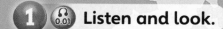 Listen and look.

2  Listen and repeat. Then match.

1

2

3

4

5

6

7

8

9

10

a Brazil   b China   c Colombia   d France   e Italy   f Mexico
g Russia   h Spain   i the United Kingdom   j the United States

3  Listen and answer the questions. Then practise with a friend.

Which country has got a yellow, blue and red flag?   Colombia!

4 Which countries do you want to visit? Ask and answer.

5 🎧 0.04 **Read and listen.**

Jules and Denis: We're from France.

Rosa: I'm from the United States, but my father's from Spain.

Maria: I'm from Brazil.

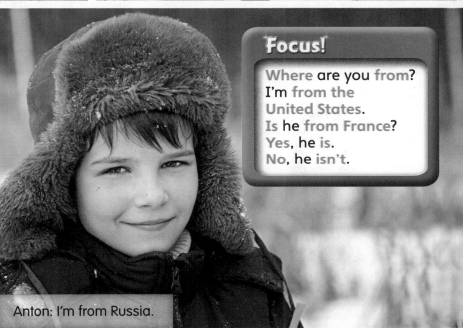

Anton: I'm from Russia.

Focus!

Where are you **from**?
I'm **from the**
United States.
Is he **from France**?
Yes, he **is**.
No, he **isn't**.

6 **Match the questions and answers. Then ask and answer.**

1 Where is Rosa from?
2 Where are Jules and Denis from?
3 Is Maria from Brazil?
4 Is Anton from Italy?
5 Where is Rosa's father from?

a He's from Spain.
b No, he isn't. He's from Russia.
c They're from France.
d She's from the United States.
e Yes, she is.

7 (My World) **Answer the questions. Then ask a friend.**

Where are you from?
Where are your friends from?

Where are your parents from?
Where are your grandparents from?

8 🎧 0.05 **Go to page 102. Listen and repeat the chant.**

→ Activity Book page 5   Grammar

Grammar fun!
▶

7

9 (0.06) **When is Carla's birthday? Listen and choose.**

a in February   b in April   c in August

10 (0.06) **Listen again and practise.**

Alex: When's your birthday, Carla?
Carla: On the 24th of April.
Alex: So is mine! When were you born?
Carla: I was born in 2006. On the 24th of April, 2006.
Alex: Oh! I was born in 2006 too!
Carla: Where were you born?
Alex: I was born in the United Kingdom. What about you?
Carla: I was born in Spain.

Focus!

1st, 2nd, 3rd, 4th, 5th, 6th, 7th, 8th, 9th, 10th
When **were** you **born**?
I **was born** on the 24**th** of April, 2006.

11 **Read about the children. Then ask and answer.**

Emma
Date of birth:
2nd June, 2005
Place of birth:
the United States

Alex
Date of birth:
24th April, 2006
Place of birth:
the United Kingdom

Carla
Date of birth:
24th April, 2006
Place of birth:
Spain

Pedro
Date of birth:
31st January, 2005
Place of birth:
Brazil

When was Alex born?   On the 24th of April, 2006.

Where was he born?   He was born in the United Kingdom.

Say it!

12 (0.07) (0.08) **How many syllables are there in each word? Listen, count and repeat.**

Spain   **birth**-day   Oc-**to**-ber

Grammar   Pronunciation   → Activity Book page 6

13 🎧 0.09 Read and listen.

WORLD QUIZ
How many questions can you answer?
A PRIZE FOR THE WINNERS!

It sounds fun! Let's do the quiz together!

Hey Ruby, look at this!

2 What's the first question, Jack?

Which city in Colombia has a flower festival?

3 My penpal, Sofia, is from Colombia! We can email her.

OK! Let's go to the reading room.

4 Where is everyone?

This isn't the reading room!

5 To win the quiz, Let's play a game. Answer the questions, And come home again.

START

Listen to this!

6 What shall we do?

Let's play the game. We want to win the quiz!

7 What's happening?

8

→ Activity Book page 7

Value: Try new things

Skills: *Listening and speaking*

Let's start! **What do people do at festivals?**

14 🎧 0.10 **Where are these festivals? Listen and match.**

a Brazil   **b** China   **c** Spain   **d** the United Kingdom   **e** the United States

1
Bonfire Night, Lewes

2
Feria, Seville

3
New Year, Shanghai

4
Carnival, Rio de Janeiro

5
Independence Day, New York

15 🎧 0.10 **Listen again and say the missing words.**
1 Bonfire night is on the 5th of   .
2 Feria is always in   .
3 Chinese New Year is in   or   .
4 The Carnival in Rio de Janeiro starts on a   .
5 Independence Day is on the 4th of   .

16 🎧 0.11 **(Talk Time) Plan a tour of some festivals.**

Which festivals would you like to go to?   I'd like to go to ...

Where are they?   The ... is in ...

Skills: *Reading and writing*

Look below! **What does Kiara want to be?**

17 🎧 0.12 **Read and listen.**

Kiara is eleven years old and she's from Moscow in Russia. Kiara wants to be a dancer. She goes to dance classes every week. She wants to dance at the Russian Winter festival.

The Russian Winter festival takes place every year in Moscow, in December and January.

Moscow is very cold in winter and there's a lot of snow. There are lots of fun activities at the festival. You can go on a troika ride through the snow. Or you can go ice-skating in the city. There are also lots of beautiful snow sculptures.

At night, you can watch the fireworks. Or you can go and see a show with traditional singers and dancers. Look out for Kiara!

18 **Read again and correct the sentences.**
1 Moscow is in China.
2 Kiara wants to be an artist.
3 The Winter festival is in November and January.
4 It is hot in winter in Russia.
5 You can go swimming in the city.
6 You can watch fireworks in the morning.

Moscow isn't in China.   It's in Russia.

Your turn!

Think of a festival you enjoy.
When is it?
Which country is it in?
What can you see there?
What can you do there?

Now write about it in your notebook.

What are **mosaics** made of?

1 0.13 **Listen and repeat.**

tiles

marble

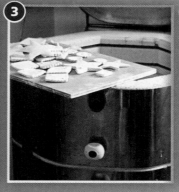
ceramic

glue

2 CLIL **Watch the video.**

3 0.14 **Read and listen.**

There are lots of different mosaics in countries around the world. Mosaics are made of many small tiles. These tiles are different shapes and colours and are made of ceramic, glass, paper or stones, like marble.

Artists put glue on mosaic tiles and then make pictures or patterns with them. Sometimes artists glue the tiles onto cardboard first, then stick the cardboard with the mosaics onto walls, floors and roofs.

In the past, mosaics in Roman gardens and baths were made of round stones or shells. Today, artists make mosaics for places like train stations and shopping centres to make them look beautiful.

Guess What!

In Spain, some artists used spoons, forks and knives in mosaics.

Let's collaborate!

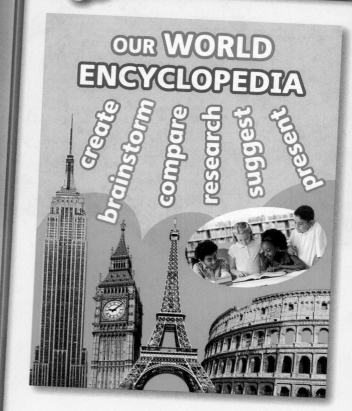

OUR **WORLD ENCYCLOPEDIA**

create brainstorm compare research suggest present

4 **Answer the questions.**

1 What type of art has many small tiles?
2 What can the tiles be made of?
3 Where were there very old mosaic floors?
4 Why do artists make mosaics today?

5 **Where would you put a mosaic in your school?**

1 Family and pets

Look!

Guess What!

1 🎧 **Listen and look.**

2 🎧 **Listen and repeat. Then match.**

1 my grandparents
2 my aunt
3 my parents
4 my uncle
5 my sister
6 my brother
7 my cousin
8 my best friend
9 my kitten
10 my puppy

a artistic   **b** clever   **c** friendly   **d** funny   **e** hardworking
f kind   **g** naughty   **h** shy   **i** sporty   **j** talkative

3 🎧 Think **Listen and guess who. Then practise with a friend.**

They're friendly.   Alex's grandparents!

4 My World **What are your family like? Ask and answer.**

5 **Read and listen.**

Focus!
My dog is cleverer than my cat.
My brother is more hardworking than my sister.

I'm more talkative than
my cousin,
She's shyer than me,
And I'm friendlier than
my cousin,
But she's kinder than me.

6 **Listen and choose the words.**

I'm **more artistic/more hardworking** than my brother,
He's **funnier/sportier** than me,
And I'm **more hardworking/more talkative** than my brother,
But he's **cleverer/kinder** than me.

7   **Make questions. Then ask a friend.**

Are you	more talkative	than your sister?
Is your brother	friendlier	than you?
Is your sister	more hardworking	than your brother?
Is your cousin	cleverer	than your cousin?
Is your friend	more artistic	than your friend?

Are you friendlier than your sister?

Yes, I am!

8 **Go to page 102. Listen and repeat the chant.**

→ Activity Book page 13   Grammar

Grammar fun!

9 🎧 1.07 **What are they talking about? Listen and choose.**

a friends   **b** height   **c** age

10 🎧 1.07 **Listen again and practise.**

Teacher: Who's taller, Carla – you or Emma?
Emma: I am!
Carla: Hmm. Let's see … I am!
Teacher: Wow! You're taller than Emma, now!
Emma: But I'm still older than you, Carla!
Teacher: And who's cleverer?
Carla: Oh, I don't know. We're both clever!

> **Focus!**
> Who's taller,
> you or your brother?
> My brother **is**.

11 **Read about Emma and Alex. Then ask and answer.**

Name: Emma
Born: 2nd June, 2005
Height: 1m, 60cm
Personality type: quiet but friendly
Likes: sport and homework

Name: Alex
Born: 24th April, 2006
Height: 1m, 52cm
Personality type: loud and funny
Likes: art and talking to my friends

artistic   funny   hardworking   old   quiet
short   sporty   talkative   tall   young

> Who's older?

> Emma is!

Say it!

12 🎧 1.08 🎧 1.09 **Which syllables sound the strongest? Listen and repeat.**

clev-er   re-**peat**   **talk**-a-tive   hard-**work**-ing

Grammar   Pronunciation   → Activity Book page 14

Skills: *Listening and speaking*

Let's start! What can you see at a circus?

14 🎧 1.11 **What's life like in a circus family? Listen and say the letters.**

Show time in the circus.

Sonia at home.

The circus at night.

Circus life is hard work!

15 🎧 1.11 **Listen again and say *true* or *false*.**

1 Sonia's twelve years old.
2 Sonia's older than her brothers and sisters.
3 Sonia's family are hardworking.
4 Sonia's grandparents are clowns.
5 Sonia doesn't go to school.

16 🎧 1.12 **Talk Time** **Ask about a friend's family.**

What's your cousin like?   He's/She's …

What are your parents like?   They're …

Skills: *Reading and writing*

 What are these children good at?

17 **Read and listen.**

Hot shots

Brad Miller and his younger sister Casey are from the United States. Brad is eleven and Casey is thirteen. They're both sporty and they're both very good at playing basketball.

Brad and Casey play in basketball teams. The other players in their teams are older and taller than them, but Brad and Casey are the star players. They practise basketball every day. One day they want to play for the LA Lakers.

Smart artists

Abby and Bianca Watson are twins. They're twelve years old and they're from the United Kingdom. They're very good at art and they like painting with bright colours. The twins sell their paintings in shops and art galleries.

This painting is by Abby. It's called *Nature*.

18 **Read again and answer the questions.**

1 Where are Brad and Casey from?
2 Who is older, Brad or Casey?
3 Are Brad and Casey hardworking?
4 Are Abby and Bianca from France?
5 Is Bianca older than Abby?
6 Where do they sell their paintings?

 Your turn!

Think of someone you know.
How old are they?
What are they good at?
What do they work hard at?

Now write about it in your notebook.

→ Activity Book page 17

How do
ant families
work
together?

1 🎧 1.14 Listen and repeat.

worker ant

colony

queen ant

drone

nest

2 CLIL ▶ Watch the video.

3 🎧 1.15 Read and listen.

Ants live in families called colonies. In each colony, ants work together in groups and help one another. Most colonies of ants live in nests and every colony has one queen ant. The queen's job is to make lots and lots of eggs for the colony.

There are also drone ants and worker ants in colonies. The drones help the queen ant to make eggs, and the worker ants do all of the other jobs. There are always lots of worker ants. Some of them make the nest and keep it clean and tidy. Other worker ants find food, like leaves, and bring it back to the nest.

Guess What!
Some ants can live for up to 30 years!

4 Answer the questions.

1 What are ant families called?
2 What does the queen ant do?
3 What do the drone ants do?
4 What do the worker ants do?

5 What do you like about working in a group?

Let's collaborate!

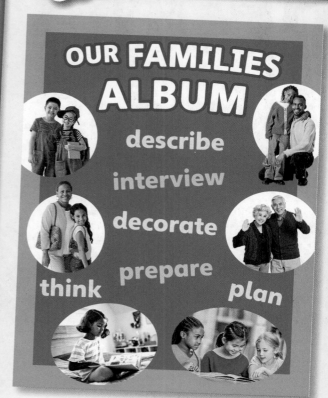

OUR FAMILIES ALBUM

describe

interview

decorate

prepare

think

plan

2 In the playground

Guess What!

1 (2.01) **Listen and look.**

2 (2.02) **Listen and repeat. Then match.**

a cry   b drop litter   c help others   d hop   e shout
f skip   g laugh   h text a friend   i throw a ball   j use a mobile phone

3 (2.03) **Listen and say the numbers. Then practise with a friend.**

They're skipping.   Number 2!

4 (My World) **What do you do at school? Ask and answer.**

5 **Read and listen.**

Our school rules

✓
- We must be hardworking and listen to the teachers.
- We must be polite and help people.
- We must put litter in the bins.

✗
- We mustn't shout in class.
- We mustn't be naughty or laugh at people.
- We mustn't drop litter on the ground.

6 **Read and say *must* or *mustn't*.**

1 We _____ do our homework.
2 We _____ eat and drink in the classroom.
3 We _____ use mobile phones at school.
4 We _____ wash our hands before lunch.
5 We _____ listen to music in the classroom.
6 We _____ be quiet in the library.

Focus!

We **must** be polite and help people.
We **mustn't** shout in class.

7 **Make school rules with a friend.**

We must play nicely with our friends.

We mustn't run in the classroom.

8 **Go to page 102. Listen and repeat the chant.**

Grammar fun!

→ Activity Book page 21   Grammar   **27**

9 (2.06) **What has Alex got in school? Listen and choose.**

a a computer game b a mobile phone c a pencil case

10 (2.06) **Listen again and practise.**

Teacher: OK, Pedro. Read us the story, please.
Alex: Oh dear!
Teacher: Alex! Have you got a mobile phone?
Alex: Yes, I have.
Teacher: You mustn't use mobile phones at school. Bring me the phone, please.
Alex: Here you are. I'm sorry.
Teacher: OK, now …
Pedro: Oh dear!

Focus!

Bring me the phone, please.
Tell the class about your holiday, please.

11 (Think) **Read and match. Then give instructions to your friend.**

1 Give Anna your book, please.

2 Bring me the ball, please.

3 Tell the class about your holiday, please.

4 Pass Max a ruler, please.

Bring me the ball, please.

Here you are.

Say it!

12 (2.07) (2.08) **Which words sound the strongest? Listen and repeat.**

Give Anna your **book**.   **Pass Max** a **ruler**.

Grammar   Pronunciation   → Activity Book page 22

13 🎧 2.09 **Read and listen.**

→ Activity Book page 23

Value: Be kind to animals

Let's start! What games do you like playing in your playground?

14 (2.10) How do you play *Queenie Queenie*? Listen and say the letters.

15 (2.10) **Put the rules in order. Listen again and check.**
a You need more than two players.
b The Queenie throws the ball behind her. She mustn't look.
c The Queenie must guess who's got the ball.
d One player is the Queenie. She takes the ball and turns round.
e Another player must catch the ball.

16 (2.11) **Talk Time** **Invent or describe a game.**

You need ... players.

You must ...

One player ...

Another player ...

→ Activity Book page 24

Skills: *Reading and writing*

 Where are these schools?

  Read and listen. Then match.

1 Kanta is from Bangladesh. Sometimes it is very rainy and the children can't go to school. So a school boat comes to Kanta's village. The boat has a classroom and a small library with computers. Pupils must study hard. Kanta studies for three hours every day. She learns Maths, Reading, Writing, English and Bengali.

a

2 Alfie is from the United Kingdom. He loves reading and he often goes to the library at his school. The library is in a bus in the playground. The bus has got two floors and there are lots of books. Pupils can also go to the library before and after school with their parents.

b

18 Read again and say *true, false* or *don't know.*

1 Kanta goes to school on a boat.
2 Alfie studies for three hours a day.
3 There isn't a library in Kanta's school boat.
4 Alfie loves reading.
5 There are computers in Alfie's library.
6 Kanta must study every day.

Your turn!
Design an unusual school. Where is it: on a boat, in a plane, in a treehouse? What subjects do the pupils study? What rules must they follow?

Now write about it in your notebook.

Where are the places on the map?

Central Park East School

Hudson River

Metropolitan Museum

Central Park Zoo

N
W E
S

Time Warner Center

32

1 🎧 2.13 **Listen and repeat.**

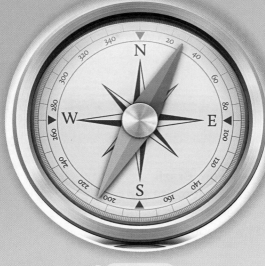

1 north

5 compass

4 west

2 east

3 south

2 CLIL ▶ **Watch the video.**

3 🎧 2.14 **Read and listen.**

A compass helps us to find places on a map. This map of *New York Central Park* shows what is in and near the park.

To the southwest of the park, we can see a big shopping centre, and we can see a zoo in the southeast. To the west of the park, there is the Hudson River. It runs from the north to the south of New York State. In the east of the park, we can see a famous museum with art from around the world. To the northeast of the park, there's a school.

This map has a compass. It shows N, E, S and W. It's easy to find places you want to visit!

4 **Answer the questions.**

1 What's to the southwest of the park?
2 Where's the Hudson River on the map?
3 Where's the school on the map?
4 What do N, E, S and W mean?

5 **When do you use a map with a compass?**

Guess What!

The very first maps showed the stars, not our world!

Let's collaborate!

SIGNS FOR OUR SUSTAINABLE SCHOOL

match   write   sketch   display   tour   discuss

→ Activity Book page 26   CLIL: Geography   **33**

Review Units 1 and 2

1  **Read, listen and choose the words.**

This is my penpal Lola. She's from **Brazil/ Mexico**. We're both **eleven/twelve**, but she's **older/younger** than me. She was born on the **2nd/4th** of October and I was born on the **22nd/24th**.

Lola and I are both **sporty/artistic** and we love **painting/football**. I think she's a bit **cleverer/ kinder** than me, though.

Lola writes to me every month and she sends me photos – like this one. Sometimes we **phone/text** each other. Lola is very **funny/shy** and her letters always make me **laugh/smile**.

Lola says I **must/mustn't** visit her one day. I'd love to!

Nadia

2 **Read again and correct the sentences.**
1 Nadia is eleven years old.
2 Lola was born on the fourth of November.
3 Nadia is older than Lola.
4 Lola sends Nadia paintings.
5 Lola isn't very funny.

3 **(My World) Think of a friend or penpal. Ask and answer.**

Where's he/she from?
When was he/she born?
What's he/she like?

4 **Write about your friend or penpal in your notebook.**

5 Play the game.

17
You _____ work hard at school.

18
born? / friend / was / your / When

19
GO BACK TWO SQUARES!

20
WELL DONE!

16
GO FORWARD ONE SQUARE!

15
A _____ person likes running, hopping and skipping!

14
aunt / Mexico? / from / your / Is

13
You mustn't _____ at other people.

9
A _____ person talks a lot.

10
THROW AGAIN!

11
You mustn't _____ mobile phones in school.

12
artistic / parents / you? / more / than / Are / your

8
homework? / always / you / do / your / Do

7
START AGAIN!

6
father / the / States? / your / Is / from / United

5
You mustn't _____ litter in the playground.

START ➡ **1**

2
born / Russia? / Were / in / you

3
A _____ person often helps other people.

4
shyer, / you / your / Who / is / or / friend?

Blue
Make a question.

Orange
Say the missing words.

3 Under the sea

Look!

Guess What!

1 (3.01) **Listen and look.**

2 (3.02) **Listen and repeat. Then match.**

a crab   **b** dolphin   **c** jellyfish   **d** octopus   **e** seal
f shark   **g** starfish   **h** stingray   **i** turtle   **j** whale

3 (3.03) (Think) **Listen and guess the animals. Then practise with a friend.**

It's got grey fur. It's smaller than a dolphin.   It's a seal!

4 (My World) **What's your favourite sea animal? Ask and answer.**

5 **Read and listen.**

Dolphins are the most intelligent sea animals. They are the friendliest too.

Blue whales are the biggest sea animals. They are the heaviest and the strongest too.

Great white sharks are the most dangerous sharks, but they aren't the most dangerous sea animals.

Box jellyfish are the most dangerous sea animals.

Focus!

the strong**est**
the heav**iest**
the **most**
dangerous

6 **Read and say *true* or *false*.**

1 Blue whales are the weakest sea animals.

2 Dolphins are the most dangerous sea animals.

3 Great white sharks are the most dangerous sharks.

4 Box jellyfish are the friendliest sea animals.

7 **Make sentences about sea animals. Then talk to a friend.**

Turtles are the most beautiful sea animals.

Yes, I agree.

No, I don't agree. I think dolphins are the most beautiful.

Say it!

8 **Which syllables sound the strongest? Listen and repeat.**

Jellyfish are **dan**gerous.   **Dol**phins are in**tell**igent.

9 🎧 3.07 **What are they talking about? Listen and choose.**

a land animals   b birds   c sea animals

10 🎧 3.07 **Listen again and practise.**

Carla: Hi, Alex. What are you doing?

Alex: I'm doing a quiz about animals.

Carla: Can I help?

Alex: OK. Question one. Which sea animal is the fastest? Is it a turtle, a dolphin or a seal?

Carla: I think it's a dolphin. Yes. A dolphin.

Alex: Well done!

Carla: OK. Question two …

> **Focus!**
> Which sea animal is the fastest?
> It's a dolphin.

11 🎧 3.08 Think **Look at the quiz. Make questions and ask and answer. Then listen and check.**

Which fish is the heaviest?

It's a whale shark.

Are you an animal whizz? Try our animal quiz.

1 fish/heavy?
a) blue shark
b) whale shark
c) great white shark

2 bird/strong?
a) eagle
b) penguin
c) owl

3 land animal/strong?
a) gorilla
b) elephant
c) bear

4 land animal/tall?
a) kangaroo
b) panda
c) giraffe

5 sea animal/slow?
a) crab
b) seahorse
c) starfish

6 land animal/dangerous?
a) hippo
b) lion
c) tiger

12 🎧 3.09 **Go to page 102. Listen and repeat the chant.**

Grammar

→ Activity Book page 32

13 🎧 3.10 Read and listen.

→ Activity Book page 33

Value: Keep our seas and oceans clean

41

Skills: *Listening and speaking*

 Let's start! What can you see at an aquarium?

14 🎧 3.11 **Which animals don't they see? Listen and say the letters.**

a

See our baby dolphins.

b

Touch a stingray.

c

Feed our friendly seals.

d

Meet Otto.

e

Get close to our sharks.

15 🎧 3.11 **Listen again and say the missing words.**
1 Otto is the .... octopus in the world.
2 Ava and Paco see .... baby dolphins.
3 Ava thinks .... are dangerous.
4 The time is .... o'clock.
5 They can feed the .... at quarter past three.

16 🎧 3.12 **Talk Time** **Plan a trip for this weekend.**

Where would you like to go this weekend?

I'd like to go to ...

How can you get there?

You can go by ...

Skills: *Reading and writing*

 What does the sea turtle rescue centre do?

 Read and listen.

Save Our Sea Turtles

Turtles are one of the most beautiful animals in the sea, but they are also in danger. How can we help them?

We must keep our seas clean. Turtles eat jellyfish, crabs, other sea animals and plants. Dirty seas are dangerous to turtles and the food they eat.

We must protect turtle nests. Turtles lay their eggs in nests on the beach. Sometimes birds and other animals eat the eggs or baby turtles.

Sea Turtle Rescue Centre

The sea turtle rescue centre has safe beaches for turtles and their nests. They help sick turtles in their animal hospital. Then they put the healthy turtles back into the sea. Turtles are happiest in the sea.

 Read again and answer the questions.
1. Are turtles dangerous?
2. How can we help turtles?
3. What do turtles eat?
4. Where do turtles lay their eggs?
5. What does the sea turtle rescue centre do?
6. Where are turtles happiest?

 Your turn!

Think of a sea animal.
Where does it live?
What does it eat?
Is it in danger?

Now write about it in your notebook.

→ Activity Book page 35

What is an **underwater** food chain?

1 🎧 3.14 Listen and repeat.

1 sunlight

2 producer

3 primary consumer

4 secondary consumer

2 CLIL ▶ Watch the video.

3 🎧 3.15 Read and listen.

Many plants and animals live underwater. How does an underwater food chain work? It needs sunlight, producers, primary consumers and secondary consumers.

Sunlight shines on the sea and some sunlight goes under the water. Plants use the sunlight to make, or produce, food inside their leaves. We call these plants producers.

Fish and other sea animals can't make their own food. They need to eat, or consume, plants and other fish. Some small sea animals or fish eat underwater plants. We call these fish primary consumers.

Then bigger sea animals or fish, like stingrays, eat smaller fish and other sea animals. They are called secondary consumers. Big secondary consumers like sharks eat animals like seals!

Guess What!
Great white sharks can live for up to three months without food.

4 Answer the questions.

1 What helps plants to make food inside their leaves?
2 Are producers plants or animals?
3 What do we call fish that eat plants?
4 What do secondary consumers eat?

5 Which other food chains can you describe?

Let's collaborate!

choose list research

OUR ENDANGERED SEA ANIMALS PROJECT

presentation plan decide

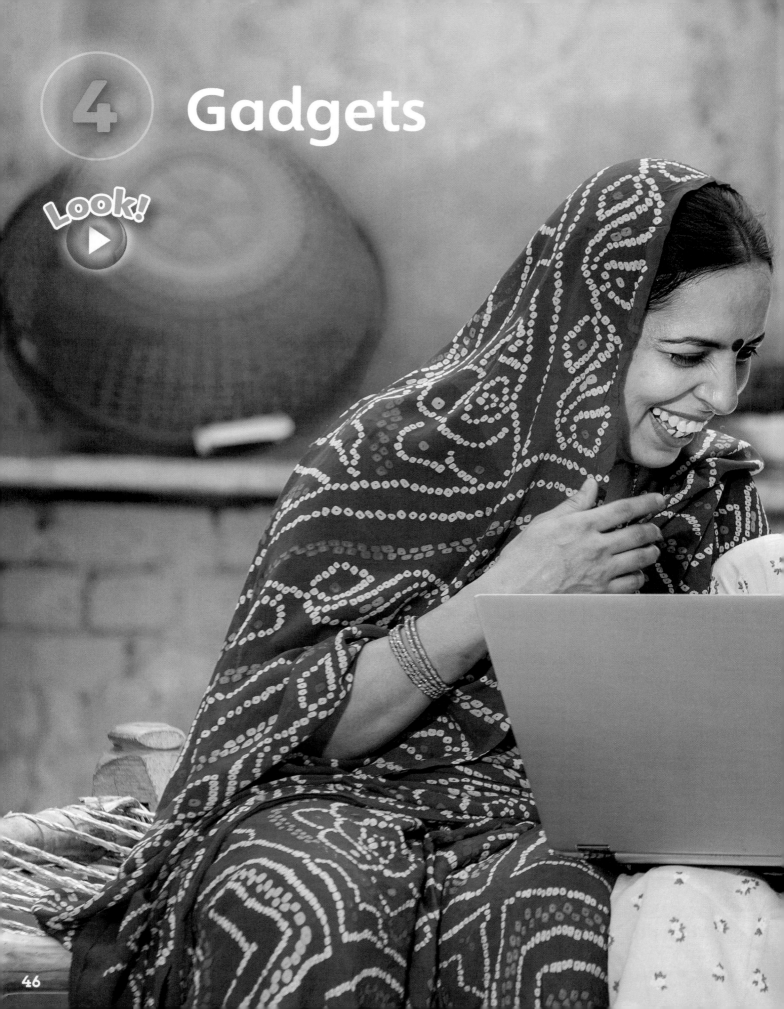

4 Gadgets

Look!

Guess What!

1 🎧 4.01 **Listen and look.**

2 🎧 4.02 **Listen and repeat. Then match.**

a digital camera   **b** e-reader   **c** games console   **d** headphones   **e** laptop
f MP4 player   **g** smartphone   **h** tablet   **i** television   **j** video camera

3 🎧 4.03 (Think) **Listen and answer the questions. Then practise with a friend.**

Can you listen to music on an MP4 player?   Yes, you can!

4 (My World) **What gadgets have you got? Ask and answer.**

5 **Read and listen.**

Luisa: I listened to music on an MP4 player in a watch!

Tia: I didn't play games or watch a film. I studied English on an e-reader.

Max and Adam: We didn't listen to music. We played great games on the consoles.

Lottie and Simon: We watched a film on a tablet. We used some cool headphones.

6 **Read and say the names.**

1 They played on the games consoles.
2 She didn't watch a film.
3 She used an e-reader.
4 She listened to music on an MP4 player.
5 They didn't play on the games consoles. They watched a film.

Focus!

I **studied** English.
I **listened** to music on an MP4 player.
We **didn't listen** to music.

7 **My World** **Make true and false sentences about you. Then talk to a friend.**

listened to	a games console	yesterday evening
watched	my MP4 player	last night
played on	television	last Saturday
used	my laptop	this morning before school

I watched television this morning before school.   False.

8 **Go to page 102. Listen and repeat the chant.**

9 (4.06) **Who did Emma visit last weekend? Listen and choose.**

a her cousins b her friends c her grandparents

10 (4.06) **Listen again and practise.**

Carla: Hi, Emma. What did you do last weekend?
Emma: I visited my grandparents.
Carla: Was it fun?
Emma: Yes, it was great.
Carla: What did you do?
Emma: We watched television and we played on their new games console.
Carla: Have your grandparents got a games console?
Emma: Yes, they have. They love playing games!

Focus!

What **did** you **do** last weekend? I **visited** my grandparents.

11 (My World) **Choose four activities you did last weekend. Then talk to some friends.**

What did you do last weekend?

I played football.

So did I.

I didn't. I visited my cousins.

listened to music | played with friends | played football | phoned a friend | used a laptop

played on a games console | tidied my room | painted a picture

helped my parents | watched television | walked in the park | studied English

Say it!

12 (4.07) (4.08) **Can you hear the different endings? Listen and repeat.**

/d/	/t/	/id/
played	watched	visited

Grammar   Pronunciation   → Activity Book page 40

Skills: *Listening and speaking*

Let's start! Which gadgets have you got?

14 🎧 4.10 **What were the first gadgets? Listen and match.**

Adam Osborne   Martin Cooper   Ralph Baer

a

b

c
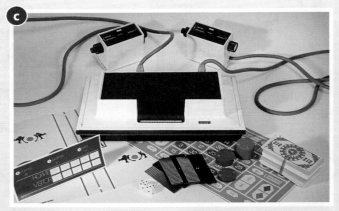

1973   1981   1967–1968

15 🎧 4.10 **Listen again and answer the questions.**

1 What was the name of the first games console?
2 How many games were there on the first games console?
3 What was the name of the first laptop?
4 How long was the first mobile phone?
5 Where did Martin Cooper get the idea for a mobile phone?

16 🎧 4.11 **Talk Time** **Decide which inventions are the most useful.**

Which invention is the most useful?   I think it's the …

What do you use it to do?   I use it to …

Skills: *Reading and writing*

 Look below! **What does Max like using his smartphone for?**

17 **Read and listen.**

Max is eleven years old and he likes making films with his smartphone. We asked him some questions.

How do you make films?
I think of a story with my friends. Then they act out the story and I film it.

Where do you make your films?
We usually go to the park and make the film outside. Then we go home and edit the film on my laptop. Editing means choosing the best parts of the film. I add music and special effects on my laptop, too.

Where do you watch your films?
On the laptop. Sometimes our parents watch them. They think the films are funny.

Is making films difficult?
No. It's easy with a smartphone!

18 **Read again and correct the sentences.**
1   Max is twelve years old.
2   He likes making films with his digital camera.
3   He makes films with his cousins.
4   He always makes films in the park.
5   He edits the films on a games console.
6   His parents think the films are boring.

Your turn!
Think of your favourite gadget.
What is it?
What do you like doing with it?

Now write about it in your notebook.

How do we read a line graph?

1 🎧 4.13 Listen and repeat.

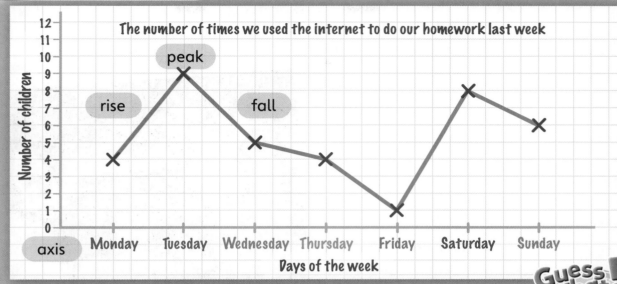

The number of times we used the internet to do our homework last week

rise · peak · fall · axis

Number of children / Days of the week

Mon	Tues	Wed	Thurs	Fri	Sat	Sun

data

Guess What!

Different names for the number 0 include zero, nought, zilch and zip.

2 CLIL ▶ Watch the video.

3 🎧 4.14 Look at activity 1. Listen and read the data on the line graph.

4 Answer the questions.

1 How many children used the internet to do their homework on Wednesday?
2 When was there a big rise in the number of children using the internet?
3 When was there a bigger fall – between Tuesday and Wednesday or between Thursday and Friday?
4 Which day shows the peak number of children using the internet?

5 What different data can you put in a line graph?

Let's collaborate!

OUR SCREEN TIME SURVEY

list · ask · record · recommend · conclude · bar chart

Review Units 3 and 4

1 🎧 **4.15** **Read, listen and choose the words.**

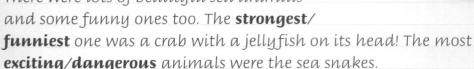

On my eleventh birthday, I **visit/visited** my favourite **art gallery/cinema** in London with my family. The cinema has got the **biggest/smallest** screen in the United Kingdom and it was great. We watched a very **dangerous/ interesting** film. It was called *Under the Sea*. The film was in 3D and we **need/ needed** special **headphones/glasses**. There were lots of beautiful sea animals and some funny ones too. The **strongest/ funniest** one was a crab with a jellyfish on its head! The most **exciting/dangerous** animals were the sea snakes. We also **listened/learned** about looking after our oceans. We must keep them **clean/dirty**. It was my favourite birthday ever!
Tom

2 **Read again and answer the questions.**

1 How old was Tom?
2 Where did he visit on his birthday?
3 What film did he watch?
4 What was the funniest sea animal?
5 What did Tom learn about oceans?

3 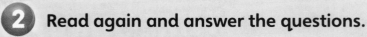 **Think of a visit to the cinema. Ask and answer.**

What film did you watch?
Was it in 3D?
What was it about?

4 **Write about a cinema visit in your notebook.**

→ Activity Book page 46

5 Play the game.

TECHNOLOGY ⚡ FAIR ⚡

① Start

④ Free headphones! Miss a turn!

③ watch television/ last night

② Which is the strongest land animal?

⑤ use an e-reader/ before school

Which sea animal has got eight legs?

⑦ visit grand-parents/last weekend

⑥ Which is the most dangerous sea animal?

Play on the games consoles! Miss a turn!

⑬ listen to music/ yesterday evening

⑪ play on a laptop/ yesterday afternoon

⑫ You lose your smartphone. Go back to the start.

Which is the most intelligent sea animal?

⑭ Which dangerous sea animal has got lots of teeth?

⑱ Finish!

⑰ study English/ last Saturday

⑯ Which is the tallest land animal?

⑮ Watch the digital jellyfish. Miss a turn!

Green
Answer the questions.

Purple
Make true sentences using these words.

57

5 The natural world

Look! ▶

Guess What!

1 🎧 5.01 **Listen and look.**

2 🎧 5.02 **Listen and repeat. Then match.**

a cave   **b** desert   **c** forest   **d** island   **e** jungle
f lake   **g** mountain   **h** river   **i** volcano   **j** waterfall

3 🎧 5.03 Think **Listen and say *true* or *false*. Then practise with a friend.**

You can climb a mountain.   True!

4 My World **Which of these things would you like to see? Ask and answer.**

What did you do in the holidays?

5 (5.04) **Read and listen.**

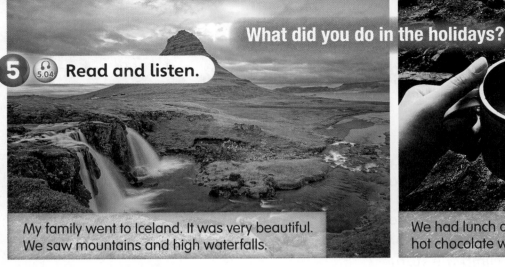

My family went to Iceland. It was very beautiful. We saw mountains and high waterfalls.

We had lunch on a volcano! We drank hot chocolate with our lunch.

We swam in a lake. The water was warm.

We caught a big fish in a river. Then we ate the fish for dinner. It was delicious.

6 (Think) **Read and correct the sentences.**

1 The family went to Russia.
2 They had lunch in a café.
3 They drank orange juice.
4 They swam in a river.
5 They caught a seal in a river.
6 They ate an octopus for dinner.

Focus!

eat – ate
catch – caught
drink – drank
have – had
see – saw
swim – swam
go – went

7 (My World) **Think about your holiday last summer. Then ask and answer.**

Where did you go on holiday last summer?
What did you do?
What did you see?
What did you eat and drink?

I went to Baha in Mexico. We swam in the sea and we saw whales. We didn't see any sharks.

Say it!

8 (5.05)(5.06) **Which words sound the strongest? Listen and repeat.**

We **didn't go** to a **mountain**.   We **went** to a **lake**.

Grammar fun!

9 🎧 5.07 **Where did Emma go on holiday? Listen and choose.**

  a a desert **b** a jungle **c** an island

10 🎧 5.07 **Listen again and practise.**

  Alex: Hi, Emma. What are you doing?
  Emma: I'm making an album of my holiday. Look, I went to Easter Island.
  Alex: Cool! Did you see these statues?
  Emma: Yes, I did. They were amazing.
  Alex: Did you climb the statues?
  Emma: No, I didn't! You mustn't climb on statues, Alex.
  Alex: I know. It was a joke!

> **Focus!**
>
> **Did** you **see** statues?
> Yes, I **did**.
> No, I **didn't**.

11 (Think) **Look at Alex's holiday scrapbook. Then ask and answer.**

| see animals   swim in a lake   climb a mountain   have a picnic   drink coffee |
| go on a boat trip   see a cave   catch a fish   take photos   visit a museum |

  Did he see animals?   Yes, he did.

  Did he swim in a lake?   No, he didn't.

the mountain we climbed

my sister at our picnic

WHITE SHARK boat trip

penguins at the beach

my grandpa and grandma at the market

12 🎧 5.08 **Go to page 103. Listen and repeat the chant.**

Grammar fun!

Grammar

→ Activity Book page 50

13 🎧 5.09 **Read and listen.**

1 Help! I can't see anything. I don't like the dark!

Which country is Hollywood in? ???

Don't worry, Ruby. We can use the tablet.

2 We're in a cave.

How do we get out?

Let's try this path.

3 Oh, no! I don't like bats.

Don't worry, Sofia.

Let's try the other path.

4 Wow!

Cut!

5 We're very sorry!

Oh, dear!

Don't worry! You can help us.

SCRIPT

DIR

6 Four actors didn't come this morning.

HOLLYWOOD

We're in Hollywood, in the United States!

7 Oh dear! I'm not good at acting.

You're a great actor, Jack!

Action!

8 That was great!

And cut! Thank you everyone.

→ Activity Book page 51

Value: Encourage your friends

63

Let's start! What is the most interesting animal you can think of?

14 🎧 5.10 **Where can you find them? Listen and say *rainforest* or *desert*.**

bilby

armadillo lizard

rafflesia

parrot flower

baseball plant

15 🎧 5.10 **Listen again and choose the words.**

1 Bilbys have long **ears/legs**.
2 Armadillo lizards are **big/small**.
3 The rafflesia is the **oldest/biggest** flower in the world.
4 The parrot flower looks like a **bird/bat**.
5 The baseball plant grows in **the United States/China**.

16 🎧 5.11 **Talk Time** **Identify animals and plants.**

What's this animal called?

It's called a ...

What's this plant called?

It's called a ...

Skills: *Reading and writing*

   What did Billy do on holiday?

17 🎧 5.12 **Read and listen.**

My holiday in the Volcanoes National Park.

We arrived yesterday. The park is very beautiful. There are mountains, volcanoes and rainforests. There are also about 480 mountain gorillas in the park. We wanted to see them.

You can only visit the gorillas with a guide. We got up very early this morning and walked through the forest for three hours. Then our guide pointed in front of us. We saw a gorilla family!

There was a mother gorilla with a baby and a father gorilla. Father gorillas are called silverbacks and they are very strong. The gorillas didn't hide, they watched us too! We stayed near them for one hour. Then we went back to our hotel. It was the most exciting day of my life!

18 **Read again and answer the questions.**
1 Did Billy go to a desert?
2 How many gorillas live in the park?
3 Did Billy visit the gorillas at night?
4 What are father gorillas called?
5 Were the gorillas interested in Billy?
6 Did he enjoy meeting the gorillas?

Your turn!

Think of your favourite holiday.
Where did you go?
What did you do?
What did you see?

Now write about it in your notebook.

What happens when a volcano erupts?

1 🎧 5.13 Listen and repeat.

① vent ② crater ③ lava ④ rock ⑤ ash

2 CLIL ▶ Watch the video.

3 🎧 5.14 Read and listen.

Volcanoes look like mountains, but volcanoes have a vent inside and a crater at the top. Sometimes they erupt and very hot, red material comes up the volcano's vent and runs into the crater. This hot material is called lava and it is very dangerous.

Next, ash and rocks fly high into the air and the lava runs down the sides of the volcano. After the eruption, the lava gets colder and it turns to rock.

Lava sometimes runs over plants and then they stop growing.

A volcano that erupts is called an active volcano. There are about 1500 active volcanoes in the world.

Guess What!

The world's largest active volcano is Mauna Loa in Hawaii. It is 4,169 m tall.

4 Answer the questions.

1 What does a volcano look like?
2 What is at the top of the volcano?
3 What happens to the very hot, red material when a volcano erupts?
4 How many active volcanoes are there?

5 Which volcano would you like to see?

Let's collaborate!

✓ OUR NATURAL WORLD QUIZ ✗

answer   decide
assign
false   revise
true

6 Helping at home

Look!
▶

Guess What!

1 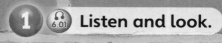 **Listen and look.**

2 (6.02) **Listen and repeat. Then match.**

a clean the bathroom   **b** cook dinner   **c** dry the dishes   **d** lay the table
e make my bed   **f** put the rubbish out   **g** sweep the floor
h tidy my bedroom   **i** wash my clothes   **j** water the plants

3 (6.03) Think **Listen and guess the answers. Then practise with a friend.**

What's he doing?   Hmm … he's putting the rubbish out!

4 My World **How often do you help at home? Ask and answer.**

5 🎧 6.04 **Read and listen. Then read and say the names.**

TUESDAY
- Ellen — please tidy your room and lay the table.
- Alfie — please make your bed and water the plants.
- Max — please put the rubbish out and sweep the floor.
- Thanks, Mum

1 I have to water the plants and I have to make my bed. I don't have to put the rubbish out.

2 My sister has to tidy her room and she has to lay the table. She doesn't have to make her bed.

3 My brother doesn't have to tidy his room. He has to sweep the floor and he has to put the rubbish out.

Focus!

I **have to** make my bed.
I **don't have** to put the rubbish out.

6 **Read and answer the questions.**

1 Does Ellen have to make her bed?
2 Does Max have to tidy his room?
3 Does Alfie have to put the rubbish out?

4 Does Ellen have to lay the table?
5 Does Max have to sweep the floor?

7 Think **Write an instruction for a friend. Then mime and guess.**

Please clean the bathroom.   Do you have to clean the bathroom?   Yes, I do.

Say it!

8 🎧 6.05 🎧 6.06 **Can you hear the different endings? Listen and repeat.**

/s/	/z/	/iz/
plants	clothes	dishes

Grammar fun!

9 🎧 6.07 **What does Pedro like doing? Listen and choose.**

a collecting the books   **b** watering the plants
c feeding the fish

10 🎧 6.07 **Listen again and practise.**

Alex: What do you have to do today, Pedro?
Pedro: I have to collect the books. What about you?
Alex: I have to water the plants.
Pedro: Who has to feed the fish today?
Alex: Emma does.
Pedro: Lucky her – I love feeding the fish.
Who has to feed the fish tomorrow?
Alex: You do.
Pedro: Oh, good!

> **Focus!**
>
> What **do** you **have to do**?
> I **have to** collect the books.
> Who **has to** feed the fish?
> Emma **does**.

11 (Think) **Look at the classroom rota.
Then ask and answer.**

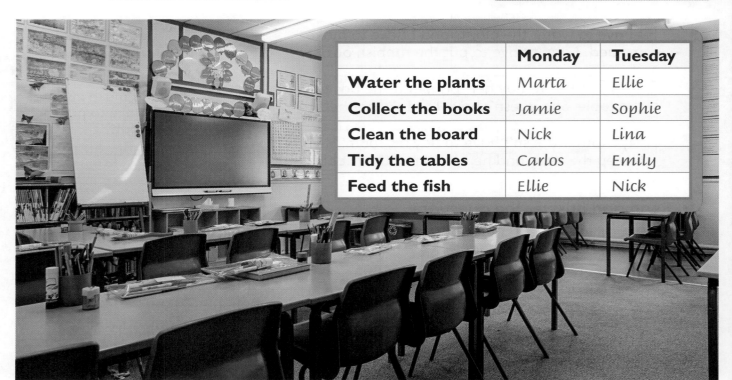

	Monday	**Tuesday**
Water the plants	Marta	Ellie
Collect the books	Jamie	Sophie
Clean the board	Nick	Lina
Tidy the tables	Carlos	Emily
Feed the fish	Ellie	Nick

Who has to clean the board on Monday?   Nick!

What does Nick have to do on Tuesday?   He has to feed the fish.

12 🎧 6.08 **Go to page 103. Listen and repeat the chant.**

    Grammar   → Activity Book page 58

13 🎧 6.09 **Read and listen.**

Which river flows through Egypt? ? ? ?

It's a palace in Ancient Egypt!

This must be the River Nile.

2 What's wrong?

The King wants to visit today. We have to finish the palace!

We can help.

4 It's beautiful!

Thank you for your help!

5 Look! The King is coming.

6 Oh dear! Where's the key to the palace!

7 Capu! Stop!

No, it's OK. He's a clever monkey!

8 Welcome, King!

It was the key!

Well done, Capu!

→ Activity Book page 59

Value: Help other people

73

Skills: *Listening and speaking*

Let's start! What does your home look like?

14 🎧 6.10 **Where do these families live? Listen and say the letters.**

a

b

c

d

15 🎧 6.10 **Listen again and say *true* or *false*.**

1   The transparent house is in Japan.
2   The cave house hasn't got a bathroom.
3   The family with the houseboat live in the United Kingdom.
4   Six giraffes live at the Giraffe Manor hotel.

16 🎧 6.11 **(Talk Time) Design your own home.**

It's a cave house. It's got …

There are … bedrooms.

The living room is …

The garden's got …

Skills: *Reading and writing*

 Look below! **What does Sasha do to help at home?**

17 (6.12) **Read and listen.**

Sasha Rudd lives on a farm.
What does she have to do at home?

I get up at six o'clock in the morning and I help with the animals. We've got cows, goats and hens on our farm.

I feed the hens every morning before school. I have to collect the eggs too. This morning I found six eggs. We had them for breakfast.

At the weekend, I help with the goats. I have to feed them and I milk them, too. We make cheese with the milk.

I don't have to help with the cows much, but sometimes I have to clean the cowshed after school. That isn't my favourite job!

Life on a farm is hard work, but it's fun. Come and stay!

18 **Read again and say the missing words.**
1 Sasha ▢▢▢▢ ▢▢▢▢ at six o'clock in the morning.
2 There are cows, ▢▢▢▢ and goats on Sasha's farm.
3 Sasha had eggs for ▢▢▢▢ this morning.
4 Sasha helps with the ▢▢▢▢ at the weekend.
5 Sasha's family make ▢▢▢▢ with goat's milk.
6 Sasha has to ▢▢▢▢ the cowshed after school.

Your turn!

Think about your day.
What do you do before and after school?
Do you have to help at home or school?

Now write about it in your notebook.

→ Activity Book page 61

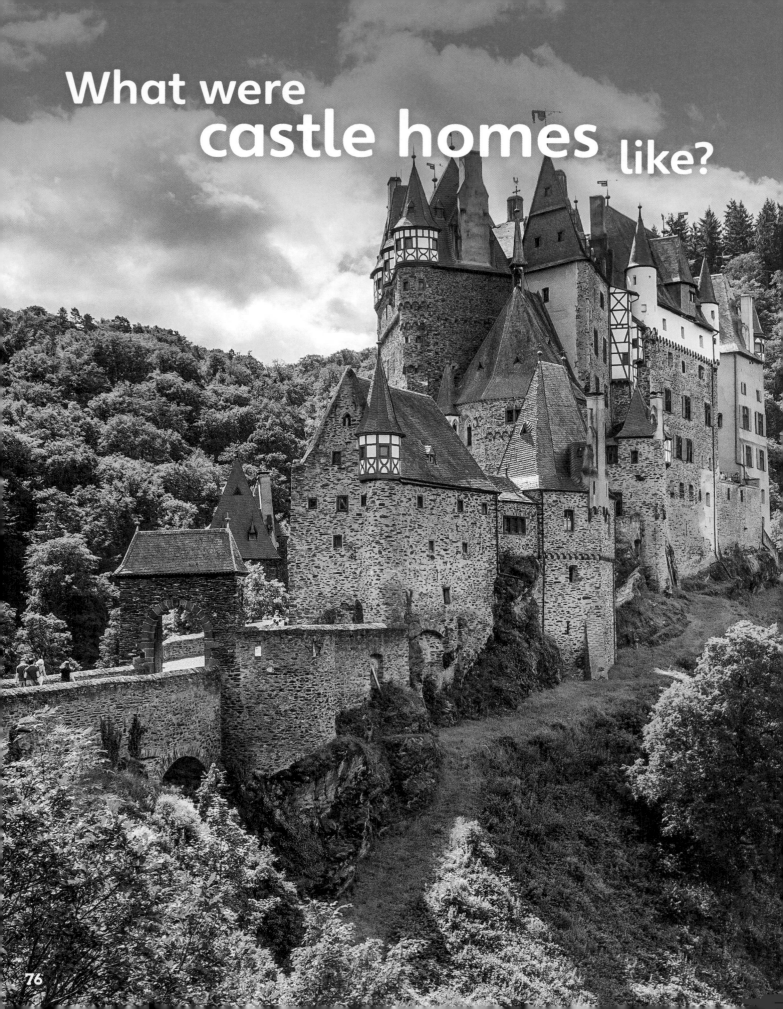

What were castle homes like?

1 🎧 6.13 Listen and repeat.

tower

candle

fire

wall

2 CLIL ▶ Watch the video.

3 🎧 6.14 Read and listen.

In the past, some people lived in castles. Most castles had water and big walls around them. The castle walls had tall towers in them. People climbed the towers to see things far away.

Inside the castle there was one very big hall. In this room, families had meals around a long, wooden table and talked and listened to music.

Castles had very big kitchens and people cooked food on open fires. People ate a lot of meat and also bread, fruit and vegetables. Castles had big gardens and people grew their own fruit and vegetables. It was very dark at night, and there were no lights. People used candles to see in the dark.

Guess What!
People used wood, not stone, to make the very first castles.

4 Answer the questions.

1 Where did families eat, talk and listen to music?
2 How did people cook their food?
3 What did people grow in the garden?
4 How did people see in the dark?

5 Would you like to live in an old castle?

Let's collaborate!

summarise · interview

OUR PLAN TO
HELP MORE AT HOME

commit · tidy up · present · compare

Review Units 5 and 6

1 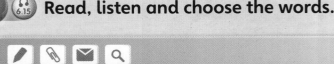 **Read, listen and choose the words.**

To:

Last month, I went to Loch Ness with my youth club. Loch Ness is a big **island/ lake** in **Russia/Scotland**. Some people think a **monster/whale** lives in it. It was an exciting weekend. Some of my friends swam in the lake, but I didn't. The water was very **hot/cold**. We all went on a boat trip and we looked for the **whale/monster**, but we **saw/didn't see** it.

In the evening, we **went for a walk/ had a picnic** in the **mountains/forest** near the lake.

Our teacher caught a **fish/monster** and I had to help cook it for **lunch/ dinner**. Then my friend had to **dry/ wash** the dishes, but we didn't have to lay **the table/the bathroom**. We didn't have one!

Becky

2 **Read again and say *true* or *false*.**
1. Becky went to a lake.
2. Becky swam in the lake.
3. Becky didn't see the Loch Ness monster.
4. Becky had to help cook dinner.
5. Her friend had to dry the dishes.

3 **(My World) Think of an exciting trip. Ask and answer.**

Where did you go?
What did you do?
What did you see?

4 **Write about your trip in your notebook.**

78

→ Activity Book page 64

5 Play the game.

7 A _____ is a tropical forest.

7 You don't like spiders! Miss a turn.

6 family? / has / Who / cook / to / dinner / your / in

6 today? / Who / tidy / to / has / classroom / the

8 holiday? / volcano / Did / climb / on / a / you

8 sweep / before / Did / school? / you / floor / the

9 An _____ is land with water around it.

5 You have to _____ a messy bedroom.

5 You don't like bats! Miss a turn.

9 You have to _____ plants sometimes.

4 chocolate / Did / drink / hot / you / night? / last

4 eat / octopus / Did / breakfast? / for / you

Well done!

FINISH

3 You have to _____ your bed in the morning.

3 A _____ is a place under the ground.

2 rubbish / Do / out? / have / you / put / to / the

ENTER HERE

clean / bathroom? / you / have / Do / to / the

Find the hidden treasure!

1 You have to _____ dirty clothes.

1 A _____ flows from a mountain to the sea.

Green
Say the missing words.

Purple
Make a question.

7 Feelings

Look!

Guess What!

1 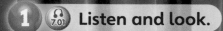 **Listen and look.**

2 (7.02) **Listen and repeat. Then match.**

a angry   **b** bored   **c** excited   **d** hungry   **e** interested
f scared   **g** surprised   **h** thirsty   **i** tired   **j** worried

3 (7.03) **Listen and say *true* or *false*. Then practise with a friend.**

Look at picture ten. She's scared.   False!

4 (My World) **Mime a feeling. Ask and answer.**

5 (7.04) **Read, listen and find. Then say the names.**

Focus!
He's scared because he doesn't like spiders.

Jim

Ben

Ali

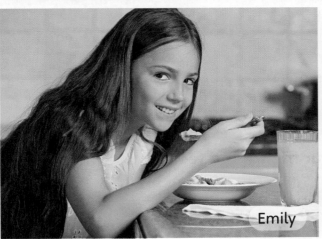

Emily

Daisy

Lucy

1 He's scared because he doesn't like spiders.
2 She's eating because she's hungry.
3 They're smiling because they're happy.

4 He's surprised because there's a spider.
5 He's laughing because it's funny.

6 Think **Read and match.**

1 Lucy is happy because …
2 Ben is suprised because …
3 Emily is hungry because …
4 Ali is scared because …
5 It's funny because …

a there's a bird on Jim's head.
b the spider is on his bananas.
c it's breakfast time.
d he really doesn't like spiders.
e she's talking to her friend.

7 My World **Make sentences with a friend.**

I'm hungry because …

I'm happy because …

Say it!

8 (7.05)(7.06) **Does the end of the sentence go up or down? Listen and repeat.**

I'm surprised because this lesson is easy. ↘ He's laughing because it's funny. ↘

→ Activity Book page 67   Grammar   Pronunciation

Grammar fun!

83

9 (7.07) **Who's scared of sharks? Listen and choose.**
   a Emma   **b** Emma's sister   **c** Pedro

10 (7.07) **Listen again and practise.**

Pedro: Hi, Emma. How are you today?
Emma: I'm OK, but I'm a bit tired.
Pedro: Why are you tired?
Emma: I'm tired because it was my sister's birthday yesterday. We stayed up late and watched a film.
Pedro: That sounds like fun.
Emma: Yes, but then my sister didn't want to go to bed because she was scared.
Pedro: Why was she scared?
Emma: Because it was a film about sharks. She's scared of sharks.
Pedro: Oh dear!

> **Focus!**
> **Why** is she tired?
> She's tired **because** she stayed up late.

11 My World **Read and match. Then ask how your friends are feeling and why.**

Why is he thirsty?

Why is she worried?

Why is she excited?

Why is he bored?   Why is she interested?

a Because there isn't any juice.
b Because he doesn't like reading.
c Because it's her birthday.
d Because she's reading a good book.
e Because the biscuits aren't on the plate.

12 (7.08) **Go to page 103. Listen and repeat the chant.**

Grammar

→ Activity Book page 68

13 (7.09) **Read and listen.**

Where does the Annatto plant grow?

Why is Capu so excited?

We're in the rainforest in South America.

Because this is his home!

2 Let's follow Capu!

Ow!

What's the matter, Jack?

...was a ...ke!

Don't be scared.

...Ve'll help.

4 We need the Annatto plant. It grows here.

ANNATTO PLANT

Can you show us, Capu?

5 Can you help us?

Of course. What's the matter?

Thank you!

→ Activity Book page 69

7 Are you OK, Jack?

Yes! They made a medicine with the plant.

8 Goodbye, Capu!

We'll miss you!

Value: Respect nature   85

Skills: *Listening and speaking*

Let's start! **What is your favourite book and why?**

14 🎧 7.10 **What are their favourite books? Listen and match.**

a **Goodnight Mr Tom,** Michelle Magorian

b **Horrid Henry,** Francesca Simon

Ben   Amber   George   Zoe

c **Charlie and the Chocolate Factory,** Roald Dahl

d **Stay Out of the Basement,** R. L. Stine

15 🎧 7.10 **Listen again and choose the words.**
1 *Stay Out of the Basement* is about two children and their **mother/father/uncle**.
2 The *Horrid Henry* stories are **exciting/funny/sad**.
3 **Four/Five/Six** children visit the factory in *Charlie and the Chocolate Factory*.
4 *Goodnight Mr Tom* is about a boy and an old **man/woman/horse**.

16 🎧 7.11 **Talk Time** **Discuss your favourite author.**

Who's your favourite author?

My favourite author is ...

What kind of stories does he/she write?

He/she writes ...

 → Activity Book page 70

Skills: *Reading and writing*

 Look below! **What is Jack climbing?**

17 **Read and listen.**

Jack and the Beanstalk

Jack and his mother lived in a village. His mother was often worried because they didn't have any money. One day, Jack had to go to the market and sell their cow. Then he had to buy some food, but Jack only bought five beans.

Jack's mother was very angry. She threw the beans out of the window. That night, they grew into a magic beanstalk. Jack and his mother were very surprised.

Jack climbed up the beanstalk. A giant lived in a castle at the top. Jack was scared but the giant was friendly. He gave Jack a magic hen for his mother. The hen made gold eggs. Jack's mother was very happy and Jack and the giant were friends.

18 **Read again and answer the questions.**
1 Why was Jack's mother often worried?
2 Where did Jack have to sell the cow?
3 How many beans did Jack buy?
4 Who lived at the top of the beanstalk?
5 Why was the hen magic?
6 How did his mother feel at the end of the story?

Your turn!

Think of a story you know.
Who is in the story?
What happens in the story?
Is the story funny, exciting, sad or scary?

Now write about it in your notebook.

How do animals communicate?

1 🎧 (7.13) **Listen and repeat.**

 growl

 flap

 hiss

 purr

 change colour

2 CLIL ▶ **Watch the video.**

3 🎧 (7.14) **Read and listen.**

Different animals communicate in different ways. Many animals use sounds to communicate with each other. Birds sing, lions and tigers growl, and tortoises can hiss. Chimpanzees touch hands to say *hello!* Some animals, like frogs and spiders, change colour to send messages to each other.

Animals communicate how they feel with their bodies, heads, mouths and ears. Animals show they are happy in different ways. Polar bears move their heads from side to side, some wild cats purr, and excited elephants flap their ears.

Animals show they are angry in different ways, too. Elephants move very fast, bears growl, and snakes and crocodiles hiss.

4 **Answer the questions.**

1 How do chimpanzees say *hello*?
2 How do some frogs and spiders send messages to each other?
3 What body parts do animals use to communicate?
4 How do snakes and crocodiles show they're angry?

5 **How do you communicate your feelings to your family?**

Guess What! Whales jump out of the water to send messages to other whales.

Let's collaborate!

OUR FEELINGS COLLAGE
organise · describe · gather · ask and answer · events · excited

Guess What!

1 🎧 8.01 **Listen and look.**

2 🎧 8.02 **Listen and repeat. Then match.**

a bodyboarding **b** canoeing **c** go-karting **d** hiking **e** rock-climbing
f rowing **g** scuba diving **h** snorkelling **i** trampolining **j** windsurfing

3 🎧 8.03 **Listen and answer the questions. Then practise with a friend.**

Look at picture five. Are they canoeing?

No, they aren't!

4 **My World** **What activities would you like to do? Ask and answer.**

5 (8.04) **Read and listen.**

Sam: It was my birthday on Saturday. I went go-karting with my friends. It was really exciting.

Lola: I went trampolining with my friends at the sports centre.

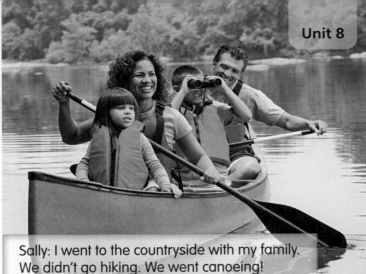

Sally: I went to the countryside with my family. We didn't go hiking. We went canoeing!

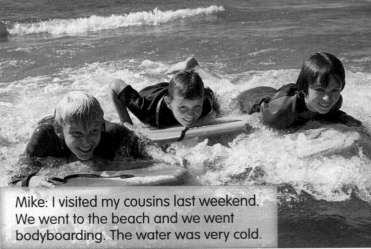

Mike: I visited my cousins last weekend. We went to the beach and we went bodyboarding. The water was very cold.

Focus!

What **did** she **do** last weekend?
She **went canoeing**.
They **didn't go go-karting** on Sunday.

6 **Match the questions and answers.**

1 What did Sam do on Saturday?
2 Did Sally go hiking?
3 Did Lola go trampolining?
4 What did Mike do?

a He went bodyboarding.
b Yes, she did.
c He went go-karting.
d No, she didn't.

7 (My World) **Ask and answer.**

What did you do last weekend?

I went hiking.

Did you go windsurfing?

No, I didn't. I went swimming.

8 (8.05) **Go to page 103. Listen and repeat the chant.**

Grammar fun!

9 🎧 8.06 **What are they talking about? Listen and choose.**

a the weekend **b** last month **c** last year

10 🎧 8.06 **Listen again and practise.**

Pedro: Can I see your photos, Carla?
Carla: Yes, of course – it's an album of my year.
Pedro: I like this photo! Did you go windsurfing last year?
Carla: Yes, I did. I went on an activity holiday with my school.
Pedro: Great. When did you go?
Carla: In March. We went rowing too.
Pedro: Cool! And when did you go skiing?
Carla: In December.
Pedro: Wow!

> **Focus!**
> When **did you go** skiing?
> I **went skiing** in December.

11 **Choose four activities you did last year. Then talk to a friend.**

snorkelling	rowing	bodyboarding
sailing	canoeing	swimming	rock-climbing
trampolining	windsurfing	ice-skating
fishing	go-karting	hiking	biking

Did you go skiing last year?   Yes, I did.

So did I. When did you go (skiing)?   In February.

Oh! I went in March.

Say it!

12 🎧 8.07 🎧 8.08 **Does the end of the question go up or down? Listen and repeat.**

When did you go windsurfing?↘   What did you do in March?↗

  Grammar Pronunciation   → Activity Book page 76

Well done, kids.
You finished the quiz.
Now off you fly,
And collect your prize.

Where can we find something to fly?

2 Look! There's a helicopter up there!

Yes, but how do we get there?

We can go rock-climbing.

OK, but we must be safe. Put on your helmets and follow me.

4 Come on, kids!

Hold on tight to the ropes.

5 It's our town!

And there's the library!

Thanks for your help, Sofia.

Do you have to go home?

Yes, I do, but it was fun!

→ Activity Book page 77

7 Goodbye, Sofia!

See you again soon!

8 Well done! How did you find out the answers?

It's a long story!

PRIZE

Skills: *Listening and speaking*

Let's start! What new hobby would you like to try?

14 🎧 8.10 **Which is Malia's club? Listen and choose a picture.**

a

b

15 🎧 8.10 **Listen again and say *true* or *false*.**

1 Malia thinks windsurfing is boring.
2 Malia goes to a windsurfing club on Tuesdays.
3 Malia has windsurfing lessons on a lake.
4 Windsurfing can be dangerous.
5 Malia gets scared sometimes.

16 🎧 8.11 **Talk Time** **Plan to join a new sports club.**

What sport shall we do?   Let's try …

What equipment do we need?   We need …

Skills: *Reading and writing*

Look below! **Why is this game of volleyball different?**

17 🎧 8.12 **Read and listen.**

Let's try something different!

Do you like trampolining? Try bossaball! Bossaball is like volleyball, but you play on a trampoline. There are two teams. The players hit or kick the ball over a net. The ball hits the floor and the team gets a point.

Can you swim underwater? What about playing hockey? Underwater hockey started in the United Kingdom. Now people play it all over the world. There are two teams. The players have to push a hockey puck at the bottom of a pool. It's also called *Octopush*.

Do you enjoy bodyboarding? Have you got a dog? How about a dog surfing competition? Dog surfing competitions are popular in California, in the United States. There are competitions every year.

18 **Read again and say the missing words.**

1 Bossaball is like _____ .
2 You play bossaball on a _____ .
3 You play underwater _____ in a swimming pool.
4 There are _____ teams in underwater hockey.
5 _____ surfing is popular in the United States.
6 There are competitions _____ .

Your turn!

Think of an unusual sport. Where do you play it? How do you play?

Now write about it in your notebook.

→ Activity Book page 79

Skills **97**

What makes our bodies move?

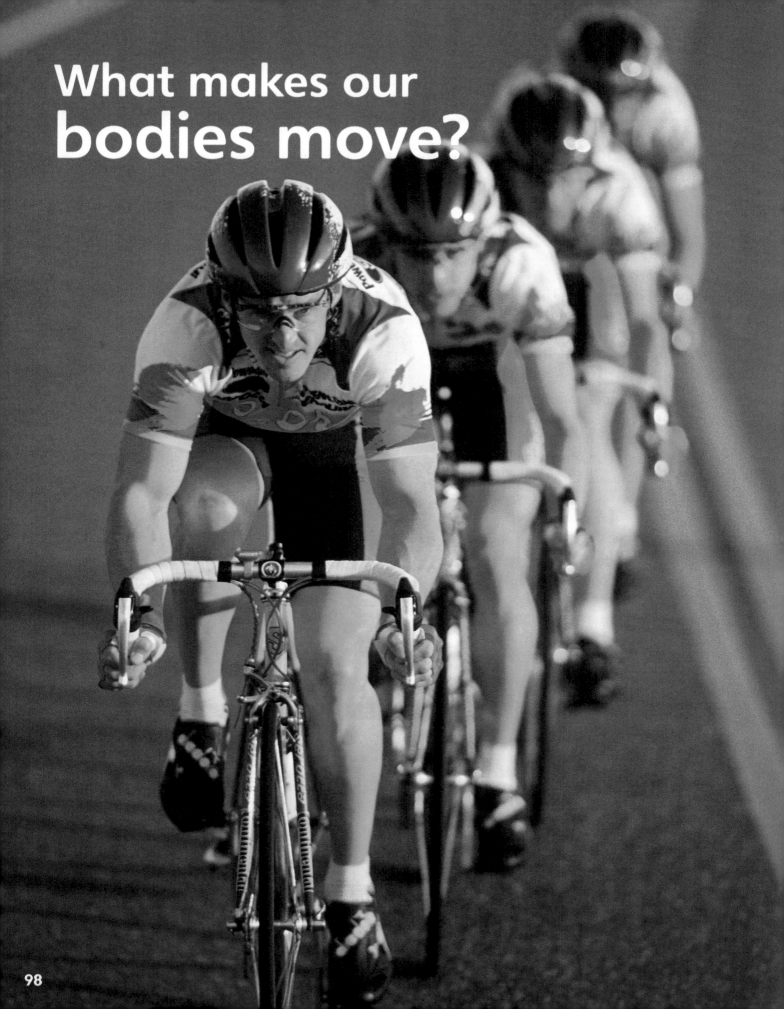

1 🎧 8.13 Listen and repeat.

1. bone
2. muscle
3. knee
4. elbow
5. joint

2 CLIL ▶ Watch the video.

3 🎧 8.14 Read and listen.

We move our bodies a lot for sport because we run, jump, bend and stretch. We use our bones, muscles and joints.

Two or more bones meet at our joints. Elbows are joints in our arms, and knees are joints in our legs. We have lots of muscles in our body, from our faces to our feet. Muscles are connected to our bones. Muscles get longer or shorter to make our joints and bones move.

We need strong bones, muscles and joints for sport. Some sports, like hiking, use our leg muscles. Some sports, like rowing, use our arm muscles. Some sports, like rock-climbing, use leg, arm and other muscles in our bodies.

4 Answer the questions.

1. What do we use to move our bodies?
2. Where are our knee and elbow joints?
3. How do our muscles help us to move?
4. Why must our bones, muscles and joints be strong?

5 Which parts of your body are the strongest and the weakest?

Guess What! We use 17 muscles in our face to smile and 43 muscles to frown!

Let's collaborate!

OUR STAY HEALTHY VIDEO

edit   think   meet   narrate   film   sports

Review Units 7 and 8

1 🎧 8.15 **Read, listen and choose the words.**

My most scary experience was last year.
I was on holiday with my parents and we went
rock-climbing/hiking in the mountains.
I was a bit **bored/excited** at first. I like **hiking/rock-climbing**, but we **climbed/walked** for a long time
and we didn't see anything.
Then suddenly we saw a brown **gorilla/bear**. It was
quite **near to/far away from** us, but I was very
excited/scared.
We were lucky **because/but** the **gorilla/bear** didn't
see us. We turned around and **walked/ran** away.
We didn't **shout/laugh** or **skip/run**.
The people at the hotel were **interested in/
surprised by** our story, but after that I didn't want
to go into the mountains again. I went **rowing/
trampolining** instead.

Josh

2 **Read again and answer the questions.**
1 Why was Josh bored?
2 Was the animal near to them?
3 Was Josh scared?
4 Did his family run away?
5 Why did Josh go trampolining the next day?

3 (My World) **Think of your most scary experience. Ask and answer.**

When did it happen?
What happened?
How did you feel?

4 **Write about your scary experience in your notebook.**

→ Activity Book page 82

5 Play the game.

START!

FINISH

1

2 Name six outdoor sports.

3 ___ did you go ___ weekend?

4 Name six feelings words.

5 ___ you bodyboarding yesterday?

6 You go back to the start because you're scared.

7 ___ do ___ did you ___ night?

8 Name six sea animals.

9 You stop because you're tired. Miss a turn.

STOP

10 Name six jobs round the house.

11 When ___ you ___ rock-climbing?

12 You stop because you're hungry. Miss a turn.

STOP

13 ___ are you tired?

14 Name six countries.

15 Did ___ teacher trampolining on Saturday?

16 Go forward two spaces.

17 Name six gadgets.

18 Why ___ your friend worried?

Blue
How many words can you remember?

Green
Say the missing words and ask a question.

Chants

Welcome (page 7)

8 **Listen and repeat the chant.**

Where are you from?
I'm from Russia.
Are you from Russia?
No, I'm not. I'm from Spain.

Where is he from?
He's from Russia.
Is she from Russia?
No, she isn't. She's from Spain.

Unit 1 (page 17)

8 **Listen and repeat the chant.**

Are you shyer than your sister?
Yes, I am.
She's more talkative than me.
Are you cleverer than your sister?
No, I'm not.
She's cleverer than me.

Is your friend sportier than you?
No, he isn't.
I'm sportier than him.
Is your friend naughtier than you?
Yes, he's naughtier than me,
My friend's as naughty as can be!

Unit 2 (page 27)

8 **Listen and repeat the chant.**

We must be polite and hardworking.
We mustn't be naughty at school!
We mustn't laugh at others.
We must be good at school!

We must listen to our teachers.
We mustn't be naughty at school!
We mustn't shout in the classroom.
We must be good at school!

Unit 3 (page 40)

12 **Listen and repeat the chant.**

Which fish is the biggest?
The biggest fish, the biggest fish?
Which fish is the biggest?
I think it's a whale shark!

Which bird is the strongest?
The strongest bird, the strongest bird?
Which bird is the strongest?
I think it's the eagle!

Unit 4 (page 49)

8 **Listen and repeat the chant.**

I didn't watch TV last night.
I played a computer game.
I used my laptop last night.
She played a computer game.

I didn't play on my tablet.
I studied for a test.
I used my new e-reader.
He studied for a test.

Unit 5 (page 62)

 Listen and repeat the chant.

Did you have a
nice time,
On your holiday?
Yes, we did – a very
nice time,
On our holiday.

Did you go on a
boat trip,
On your holiday?
No, we didn't – we
swam in a lake,
On our holiday.

Did you go on
a picnic,
On your holiday?
Yes, we did – we
ate too much,
On our holiday!

Unit 6 (page 72)

 Listen and repeat the chant.

Who has to collect the books?
Max does, Max does.
Who has to water the plant?
Kim does, Kim does.

Who has to feed the fish?
You do, you do!
I do? OK.
I'll feed the fish today.

Unit 7 (page 84)

 Listen and repeat the chant.

Why are you tired, today?
Why are you tired?
I'm tired because I stayed up late.
And now I'm very tired.

Why are you worried, today?
Why are you worried?
I'm worried because the test is today.
And now I'm very worried.

Unit 8 (page 93)

 Listen and repeat the chant.

Where did you go at the weekend?
I went to the beach with my friends.
We didn't go swimming or snorkelling.
We went bodyboarding instead.

Where did he go at the weekend?
He went to the beach with his friends.
They didn't go swimming or snorkelling.
They went bodyboarding instead.

Acknowledgements

Many thanks to everyone in the excellent team at Cambridge University Press & Assessment in Spain, the UK and India.

The authors and publishers would like to thank the following contributors:

Blooberry Design: concept design, cover design, book design
Hyphen: publishing management, page make-up
Ann Thomson: art direction
Gareth Boden: commissioned photography
Jon Barlow: commissioned photography
Ian Harker: class audio recording
Sounds like Mike Ltd: 'Grammar fun' recording
Robert Lee, Dib Dib Dub Studios: song and chant composition
Vince Cross: theme tune composition
James Richardson: arrangement of theme tune
Phaebus: 'CLIL' video production
Kiki Foster: 'Look!' video production
Bill Smith Group: 'Grammar fun' and story animations

The authors and publishers acknowledge the following sources of copyright material and are grateful for the permissions granted. While every effort has been made, it has not always been possible to identify the sources of all the material used, or to trace all copyright holders. If any omissions are brought to our notice, we will be happy to include the appropriate acknowledgements on reprinting and in the next update to the digital edition, as applicable.

Key: U = Unit

Photography

The following photos are sourced from Getty Images.

U0: Image Source; Peter Adams/The Image Bank Unreleased; Richard Sharrocks/Moment; **U1:** Wilfried Martin; elenaleonova; VStock LLC/Tanya Constantine; Marcus LindstrAm; Sviatlana Lazarenka/iStock/Getty Images Plus; LordRunar/iStock/Getty Images Plus; Fuse; TeguhSantosa/Moment; **U2:** MoreISO/iStock/Getty Images Plus; altrendo images; Alistair Berg; KidStock; Rob Friedman; Digital Vision/Photodisc; clubfoto/E+; LWA/Dann Tardif/DigitalVision; **U3:** Stephen Frink/Image Source; Rike_/E+; WaterFrame_eda; Westend61 - Gerald Nowak/Brand X Pictures; Bryce Flynn/Moment; Daniel Baumbach/EyeEm; Photo by Jocelyn Winwood, NZ. Specialist in nature shots/Moment Open; MR1805/iStock/Getty Images Plus; joebelanger; FredFroese/iStock/Getty Images Plus; paulafrench/iStock/Getty Images Plus; Nichols801/iStock/Getty Images Plus; kali9/E+; Carol Yepes/Moment Open; JulPo/iStock/Getty Images Plus; Csondy/iStock/Getty Images Plus; **U4:** Phimph Ma Yexa/EyeEm; Tara Farquhar/EyeEM; baranozdemir/iStock/Getty Images Plus; **U5:** Photography by Byron Tanaphol Prukston/Moment; Fox3X; Renata Habibullina/EyeEm; Corey Ford/Stocktrek Images; Douglas Peebles/Corbis Documentary; O. Louis Mazzatenta; **U6:** Jupiterimages/The Image Bank; WLADIMIR BULGAR/Science Photo Library; Petri Oeschger/E+; Barry Austin Photography/The Image Bank; MIXA; SolStock/E+; John Coletti/The Image Bank; SCStock/iStock Editorial; **U7:** DigitalVision/Getty; Peter Dazeley/The Image Bank; Jose Luis Pelaez Inc/DigitalVision; chuanchai/iStock/Getty Images Plus; I love nature/Moment; **U8:** mountainberryphoto/iStock/Getty Images Plus; Tom Werner/DigitalVision; Blend Images - Michael DeYoung/Tetra images; John P Kelly.

The following photographs are sourced from other libraries.

U0: Tim Gainey/Alamy; Charnsit Ramyarupa/Shutterstock; Globe Turner/Shutterstock; Paul Stringer/Shutterstock; Media Home/Shutterstock; Artgraphixel/Shutterstock; Tanya Ustenko/Shutterstock; Sporrer/Rupp/Image Source/Alamy; Radius Images/Design Pics/Alamy; RimDream/Shutterstock; Ekaterina Bykova/Shutterstock; Christine Whitehead/Alamy; SandiMako/Shutterstock; ANDRE DURAO/Shutterstock; Jose Luis Pelaez Inc/Tetra Images, LLC/Alamy; Ekaterina Bykova/Shutterstock; Norman Price/Alamy; marekuliasz/Shutterstock; Destinyweddingstudio/Shutterstock; dbimages/Alamy; BRYANT Nicolas/SAGAPHOTO.COM/Alamy; **U1:** Menzl Guenter/Shutterstock; Amir Kaljikovic/Shutterstock; Ian Allenden/Alamy; ZouZou/Shutterstock; Przemek Klos/Shutterstock; Shots Studio/Shutterstock; WEExp/Shutterstock; Vasilyev

Alexandr/Shutterstock; Anneka/Shutterstock; Q-Images/Alamy; Nick Turner/Alamy; imageBROKER/Alamy; Philippe Degroote/Alamy; elic/Shutterstock; noolwlee/Shutterstock; Johner Images/Corbis; pattara puttiwong/Shutterstock; EyeEm/Alamy; National Geographic Image Collection/Alamy; **U2:** J. McPhail/Shutterstock; Purestock/Alamy; iofoto/Shutterstock; MJTH/Shutterstock; Peter Alvey/Alamy; Cultura Creative/Alamy; Tom Wang/Shutterstock; Werli Francois/Alamy; syaochka/Shutterstock; Jon Bower UK/Alamy; David Bathgate/Corbis; Sergey Borisov/Alamy; billy bonns/Shutterstock; **U3:** Steve Noakes/Shutterstock; Kevin Schafer/Alamy; Stefan Pircher/Shutterstock; imageBROKER/Alamy; Nature Picture Library/Alamy; Christian Musat/Alamy; Nick Upton/Alamy; Zac Macaulay/Cultura RM/Alamy; Stefan Deutsch/Corbis; Carlos Villoch - MagicSea.com/Alamy; Artem Rudik/Shutterstock; **U4:** Dimple Bhati/iStock/Getty Images Plus; FERNANDO BLANCO CALZADA/Shutterstock; Jiri Hera/Shutterstock; K. Miri Photography/Shutterstock; keella/Shutterstock; Valentina Razumova/Shutterstock; neelsky/Shutterstock; Maxx-Studio/Shutterstock; Tara Farquhar / EyeEm; Igor Lateci/Shutterstock; Julien_N/Shutterstock; dpa picture alliance/Alamy; Gordon Scammell/Alamy; Goodluz/Shutterstock; Blend Images/Alamy; baranozdemir/iStock/Getty Images Plus; INTERFOTO/Alamy; Magnavox Corporation/Science and Society Picture Library; Chris Willson/Alamy; Darwin Wiggett/All Canada Photos/Alamy; Ale Ventura/Corbis; **U5:** Galyna Andrushko/Shutterstock; Pablo Hidalgo - Fotos593/Shutterstock; Andrea Willmore/Shutterstock; Filip Fuxa/Shutterstock; Chris Gardiner/Shutterstock; Dr. Morley Read/Shutterstock; lenaer/Shutterstock; Janne Hamalainen/Shutterstock; VVO/Shutterstock; Drimi/Shutterstock; javarman/Shutterstock; Robert Hoetink/Shutterstock; holbox/Shutterstock; orangecrush/Shutterstock; Eugene Sergeev/Alamy; Four Oaks/Shutterstock; Eric Nathan/Alamy; Rolf Nussbaumer Photography/Alamy; Martin Harvey/Alamy; Anthony Bannister/Avalon.red/Alamy; kkaplin/Shutterstock; WhyMePhoto/Shutterstock; Florapix/Alamy; Rolf Nussbaumer Photography/Alamy; Image Source/Alamy; Nordroden/Shutterstock; Tamara Kulikova/Shutterstock; wdeon/Shutterstock; luigi nifosi/Shutterstock; **U6:** John Birdsall/Rex; Arina P Habich/Shutterstock; Blend Images/Shutterstock; MBI/Alamy; Shotshop GmbH/Alamy; Juice Images/Alamy; tmcphotos/Shutterstock; Monkey Business Images/Shutterstock; The Photolibrary Wales/Alamy; Sergio Pitamitz/robertharding/Alamy; Aflo Co. Ltd./Alamy; Lukasz Janyst/Shutterstock; Andrey Starostin/Shutterstock; Aksenova Natalya/Shutterstock; Kletr/Shutterstock; Rob Swanson/Shutterstock; Bucchi Francesco/Shutterstock; **U7:** blickwinkel/Alamy; PathDoc/Shutterstock; Thinglass/Shutterstock; Scott E Read/Shutterstock; Martin Harvey/Alamy; Maria Dryfhout/Shutterstock; Muythaisong Pitakpong/Shutterstock; **U8:** Dimitar Kunev/Shutterstock; Zero Creative/Image Source/Alamy; stephen brian/Alamy; Robin Weaver/Alamy; imageBROKER/Alamy; Catchlight Visual Services/Alamy; BlueOrange Studio/Shutterstock; Arterra Picture Library/Alamy; Max Topchii/Shutterstock; Charles Hood/Alamy; ALAN OLIVER/Alamy; Blend Images/Alamy; Brocreative/Shutterstock; Radius Images/Alamy; RODRIGO OROPEZA/Corbis; Patryk Kosmider/Shutterstock; Matyas Rehak/Shutterstock; RODRIGO OROPEZA/Corbis; Sebastian Kaulitzki/Shutterstock; leonello calvetti/Alamy; Image Source/Alamy; BlueRing_Boumy/Shutterstock; All Canada Photos/Alamy.

Front cover Photography

Front Cover Photography by areeya_ann/500px Plus.

Illustrations

Graham Kennedy; Mark Duffin; Marcus Cutler (Sylvie Poggio); Pablo Gallego (Beehive Illustration).